microQuests

mighty
animal
cells

Rebecca L. Johnson

illustrations by Jack Desrocher

diagrams by Jennifer E. Fairman, CMI

 Millbrook Press • Minneapolis

for Mr. Wood —RLJ

Many of the photographs in this book are micrographs. Micrographs are photos taken through a microscope. Sometimes bright colors are added to micrographs to make cell parts easier to see. Other times, cells are stained with dye so cells and cell structures show up more clearly under a microscope.

As you read this book, look for the bold words in colored boxes. These words tell you about the photos and diagrams. You can also look for the lines that connect the photos and the text.

Text copyright © 2008 by Rebecca L. Johnson
Diagrams on pp. 9, 10, 17, 18, 37 copyright © 2008 by Fairman Studios, LLC
Other illustrations copyright © 2008 by Lerner Publishing Group, Inc.

Millbrook Press, Inc.
A division of Lerner Publishing Group, Inc.
241 First Avenue North
Minneapolis, MN 55401 U.S.A.

Website address: www.lernerbooks.com

Library of Congress Cataloging-in-Publication Data

Mighty animal cells / by Rebecca L. Johnson ; illustrations by Jack Desrocher ; diagrams by Jennifer Fairman.
       p. cm. — (Microquests)
    Includes bibliographical references and index.
    ISBN 978–0–8225–7137–7 (lib. bdg. : alk. paper)
    1. Cytology—Juvenile literature. I. Desrocher, Jack, ill. II. Title.
QH582.5.J64 2008
    571.6—dc22   2006036394

Manufactured in the United States of America
1 2 3 4 5 6 – DP – 13 12 11 10 09 08

table of contents

chapter 1
creating new life

The frog sperm are swimming as fast as they can. Their long tails flick back and forth. The sperm have heads but no eyes. They look like they're in a race. And they are.

Their goal is a frog egg up ahead. It's much bigger than the sperm. The egg is round like a ball. It doesn't seem to be doing anything. But it's actually sending out an invisible chemical signal. The signal guides the sperm to the egg.

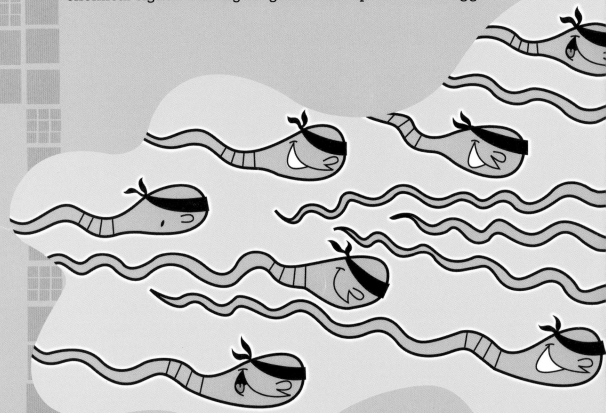

Several sperm reach the egg at *almost* the same time. At the last second, one sperm pulls ahead. In the blink of an eye, it joins with the egg. Together, the egg and sperm form a single cell.

The frog sperm comes from a father frog. The frog egg comes from a mother frog. The new cell that forms when they join will one day be a brand-new frog. This single cell is the beginning of a new life.

Every animal, plant, and person on the planet started life as a single cell. That includes you! A single cell is so small you need a microscope to see it. Cells are the smallest unit of life. They are the building blocks of all living things.

Did you know there are more than ten thousand cells in a **mosquito**? A frog or a mouse has millions of cells. Your body is made from about 100 trillion cells. That's 100,000,000,000,000!

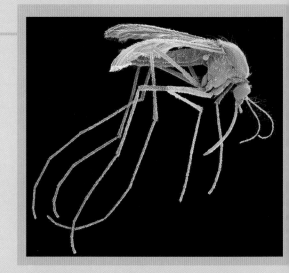

Mosquitoes, frogs, and mice are animals. People are animals too. All animals have something in common. They're made from animal cells.

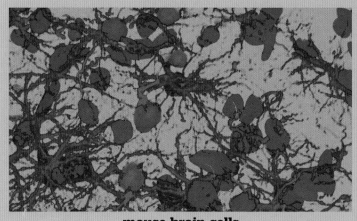

mouse brain cells

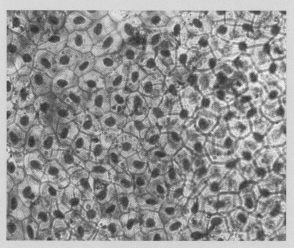
frog skin cells

When you first see an animal cell up close, it looks complicated. A single cell is made from many smaller parts called organelles. *Organelles* means "little organs." Different organelles have different jobs. But they all work together to keep the cell running.

To understand a cell, you need to get to know its parts. So let the introductions begin!

chapter 2

meet the organelles

The easiest organelle to find in an animal cell is
the nucleus. It's the dark, round shape near the center.

If cells were computers, the **nucleus**
would be the cell's hard drive. The
nucleus holds a molecule called DNA.
(That stands for deoxyribonucleic
acid.) An animal cell's DNA has all
the information to make all the
animal's cells.

Inside the nucleus, the DNA is
twisted up into **chromosomes**.
Different animals have different
numbers of chromosomes.
A frog has thirty-six. A
mouse has forty. And you
have forty-six.

Your DNA comes from the
egg and sperm that
together formed your first
cell. No one else on
Earth—unless you have an
identical twin—has DNA
exactly like yours.

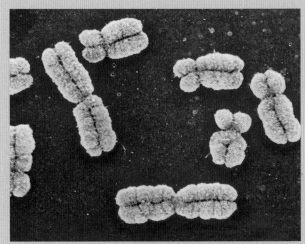

DNA tells cells how to grow and change. By controlling what cells do, it makes sure cells work together to build a whole animal.

DNA sends instructions with chemical codes. These codes are directions for making proteins. Proteins are the building blocks of cells. DNA holds instructions for making about fifty thousand different proteins. That's enough to build any animal you can think of!

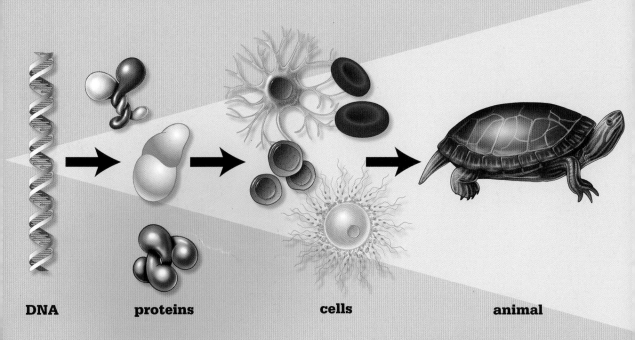

DNA   proteins   cells   animal

Outside the nucleus is a salty gel called cytosol. It surrounds the nucleus and fills the cell. All the cell's organelles float in the cytosol.

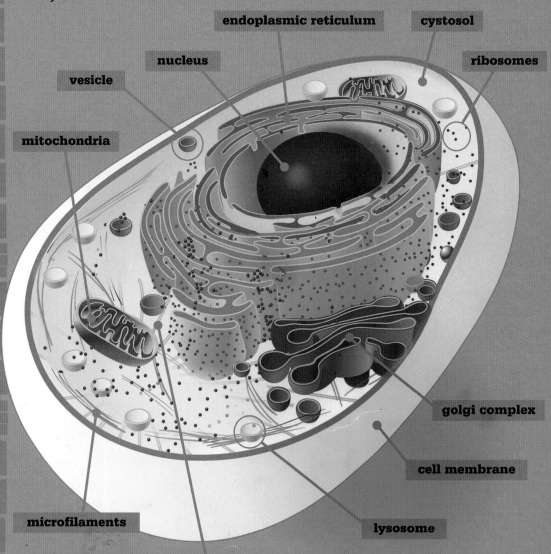

endoplasmic reticulum

cystosol

nucleus

ribosomes

vesicle

mitochondria

golgi complex

cell membrane

microfilaments

lysosome

microtubules

Ribosomes are organelles that make proteins. A cell may have hundreds or even thousands of ribosomes. DNA's chemical codes tell ribosomes which proteins to make. The ribosomes build proteins by stringing together ingredients called amino acids. It's a bit like stringing together beads to make a necklace. Lots of amino acid "beads" float around in the cytoplasm, so the cell always has what it needs.

Some ribosomes are stuck to the endoplasmic reticulum (ER). The ER is a membrane (thin structure) that weaves back and forth through the cell. New proteins move through the ER like products moving along a factory assembly line. As proteins move along the membrane, the ER makes small changes to them.

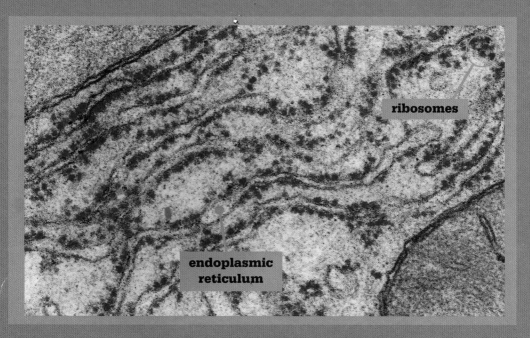

ribosomes

endoplasmic reticulum

When proteins reach the end of the ER, most go to the **Golgi complex**. The Golgi is made up of small, flattened membranes. The membranes are piled up like stacks of pancakes. Proteins are finished inside the Golgi. Then they are put into tiny sacs called vesicles.

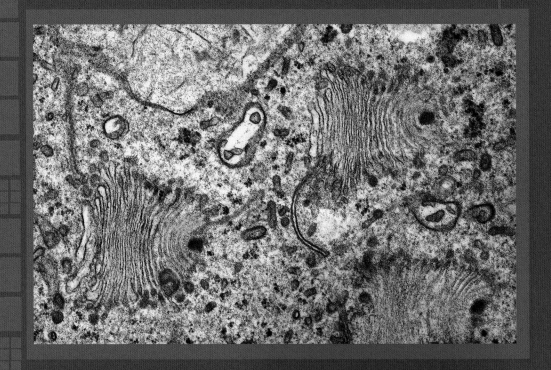

Some vesicles carry proteins to other parts of the cell. Others head for the edge of the cell and send the proteins to the outside.

Another type of vesicle buds off the Golgi. These sacs, called lysosomes, contain powerful chemicals. **Lysosomes** are the cell's cleanup crew. They find and destroy anything in the cell that's worn out or not working right.

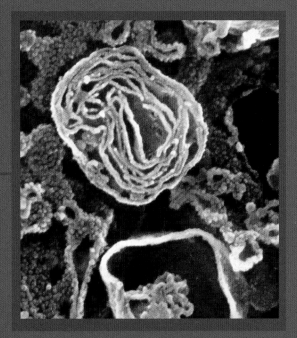

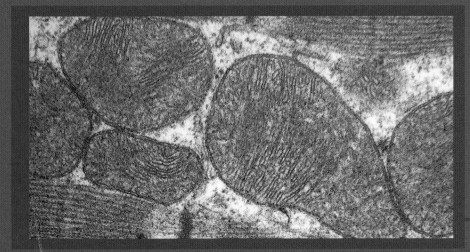

A cell does a lot of work. It needs energy to build proteins and keep on going. The energy comes from **mitochondria**. These organelles are tiny powerhouses. They change energy from chemicals into a form the cell can use.

The **cytoskeleton** does some of the same jobs as a human skeleton. It's made of long fibers (protein threads). To see these fibers, scientists stain cells in a special way.

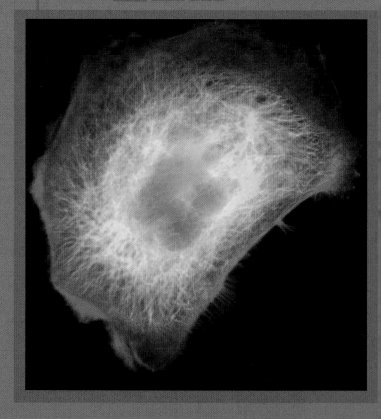

Some of the fibers in the cytoskeleton are microtubules. These fibers help support the cell from the inside. They're like bones holding up a body. Microfilaments are a second type of cytoskeleton fiber. They are mostly around the edges of the cell. Microfilaments are thinner than microtubules. They help the cell change shape.

The **cell membrane** surrounds the cell. It holds all the organelles inside. The cell membrane is more than just a covering, though. It lets some things but not others pass into or out of the cell. Protein products the cell makes are able to leave. Substances that the cell needs to live and grow are allowed to enter. But substances that might damage the cell or its organelles are never allowed inside!

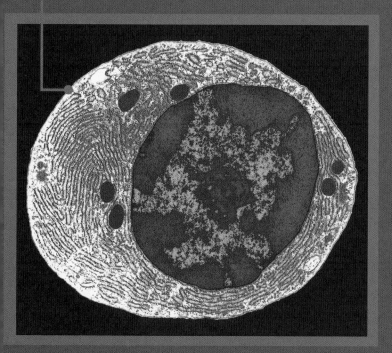

Now you know the basics of an average animal cell. Everything in the cell is controlled by DNA. But remember—that same DNA has all the information needed to build an entire animal. So let's go back to the frog cell formed by the sperm and the egg. How does a big-eyed, slimy-skinned frog develop from that single cell?

chapter 3
how cells divide

When a sperm and an egg join together, it's called fertilization. Fertilization begins a chain of events that turns one cell into millions of cells.

Most cells in a frog's body have thirty-six chromosomes. Frog sperm and frog eggs each have eighteen chromosomes. When sperm and egg join, the chromosomes are added together. That way, the fertilized egg cell has thirty-six chromosomes— exactly the right number to make a new frog.

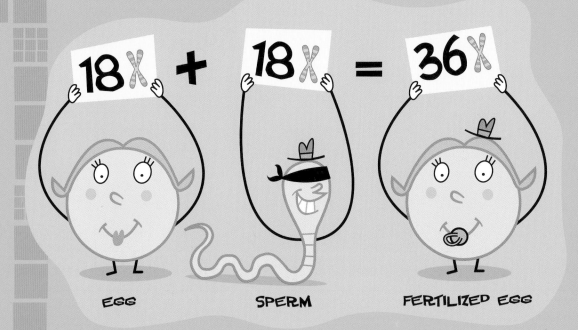

EGG   SPERM   FERTILIZED EGG

For one fertilized egg cell to become many cells, it must divide. This division is called mitosis. It happens in four basic steps. Here is how mitosis works in a cell that has four chromosomes.

In **step one**, each chromosome copies itself. The copies stay together in pairs. Two bundles of microtubules, the centrosomes, begin moving toward opposite sides of the cell. At the same time, the nucleus seems to disappear.

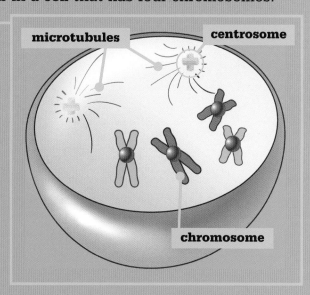

microtubules

centrosome

chromosome

In **step two**, the chromosomes line up in the middle of the cell. They seem to move as if by magic. But it's microtubules growing out of the centrosomes that pull the chromosomes into place.

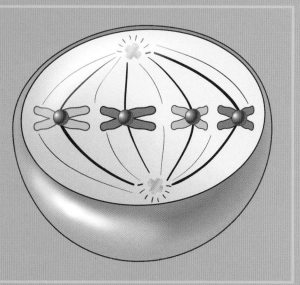

In **step three**, the microtubules begin to tug on the chromosomes. The pairs separate and are slowly pulled toward opposite sides of the cell. When the chromosomes stop moving, a new nucleus starts to form around each set.

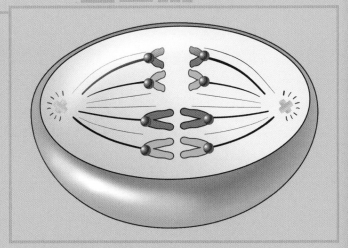

In **step four**, the whole cell begins to change shape. A crease forms in the middle. The crease gets deeper and deeper. It pinches the cell around its middle as if someone were tightening a belt around the cell's waist.

crease nucleus

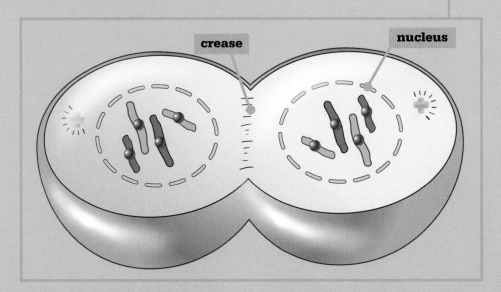

When the pinching is complete, there are two new cells. One parent cell has become two daughter cells. The two daughter cells are identical to the parent cell and to each other. They each have four chromosomes, just like the parent cell had before **mitosis** began.

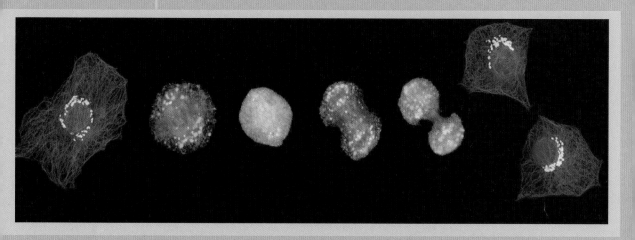

A fertilized frog egg cell goes through the same four steps when it divides. At the end of mitosis, that cell will become two cells. Those daughter cells will each have thirty-six chromosomes. And soon, they will start dividing.

The two cells divide to make four cells. Those four cells then divide to make eight. The eight divide to make sixteen, then thirty-two, then sixty-four, then 128. . . . Notice a pattern? With each division, the number of cells doubles. Soon there are hundreds, then thousands of cells.

Every time a cell divides, DNA is copied exactly. All the frog cells have exactly the same chromosomes and DNA as the very first cell.

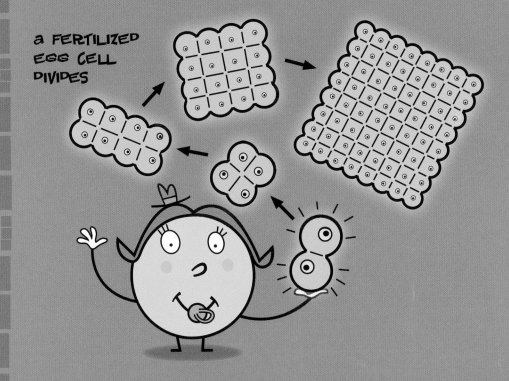

a FERTILIZED EGG CELL DIVIDES

Let's take a closer look at what happens as the **frog egg** cells keep dividing. At first, the dividing cells form a bumpy clump that looks a bit like a raspberry. After more divisions, the cells pack together to form a smoother ball.

As cell divisions continue, the cells in the ball begin to move around. Some cells on the outside sink to the inside. Some cells on the inside move out. The ball starts to hollow out.

Something else is happening too. Not all the cells in the ball are exactly the same anymore. Cells forming the outside of the ball are a little different from those in the inside.

"Now wait just a minute!" you may be thinking. "If all the cells have the same DNA, how can they be changing into different kinds of cells?"

The answer is that DNA doesn't give the same directions to all cells. Different sections of DNA turn on and off in different cells. That way, some cells build different proteins than other cells. These different cells can then do different jobs in an animal's body.

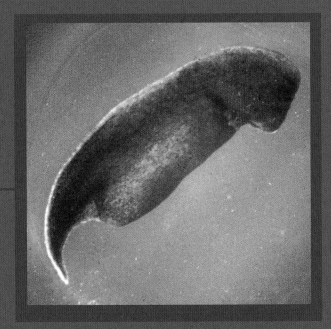

The cells in the ball keep dividing. A **tadpole body** starts to take shape. A head forms on one end. A tail develops on the other.

Other animals look very
similar at this stage.
These young, unborn (or
unhatched) animals are
called embryos. Compare
a **fish** embryo to a
chicken or a **mouse**
embryo. What do you
notice? They all have
tails, big heads, and
bumps where wings or
legs will be. As the
embryos continue to develop,
they will start looking very
different from one another.

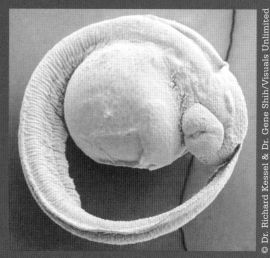

© Dr. Richard Kessel & Dr. Gene Shih/Visuals Unlimited

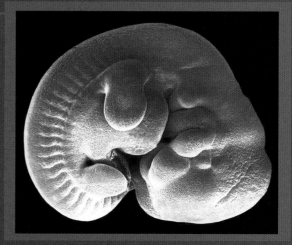

Like the frog, the fish, the chick, and the mouse, you began life as a single fertilized egg cell. That cell divided into **two cells**. Then those two cells divided again. Those cells kept dividing and changing to form a human embryo.

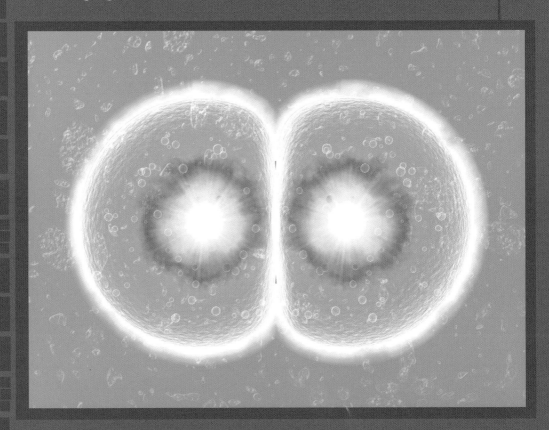

Can you guess what you looked like as an embryo? A one-month-old **human embryo** looks a lot like the embryos of other animals. You had a tail too!

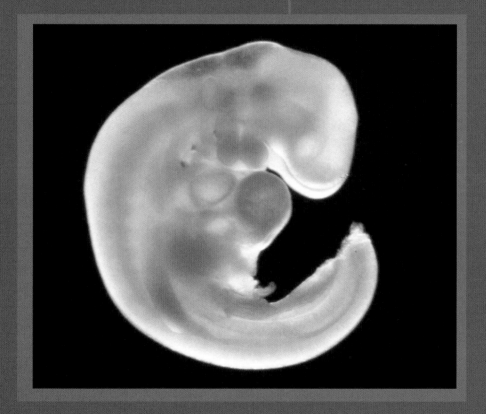

As time went on, your body began to look more human. Your tail disappeared. Your head began to look less lumpy. Your arms and legs took shape.

A frog embryo develops from a fertilized egg into a tadpole in just a week or two. Several weeks after that, it will grow legs and lose its tail to become an adult frog.

Making YOU took a lot longer. An average human baby takes forty weeks to develop. That's a little more than nine months. When you were born, you had trillions of cells in your body. Those trillions of cells can be grouped into about two hundred different kinds of cells. Each kind has a specific shape and job. Examples include skin cells, muscle cells, bone cells, and . . . wait! These cells should have a chapter of their very own.

chapter 4

what cells do

Talking about all the different types of cells in your body would take a very big book. So let's look at just a few.

Your body is covered with **skin cells**. They are tightly packed together. Your tightly packed skin cells seal water inside your body. They also keep out harmful germs.

Growing out of your skin are **hairs**. A single hair is formed from thousands and thousands of tiny, flattened cells. They overlap one another like shingles on a roof.

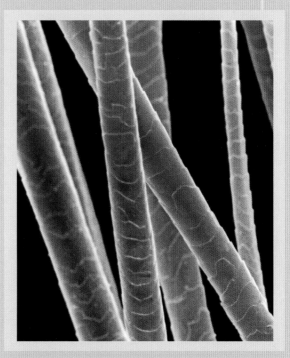

If you cut your finger, you'll bleed. In just a single drop of blood are tens of thousands of **red blood cells**. These cells give blood its red color. But their main job is to carry a life-giving gas. It's called oxygen. You take in oxygen when you breathe. Red blood cells carry it to your body's other cells.

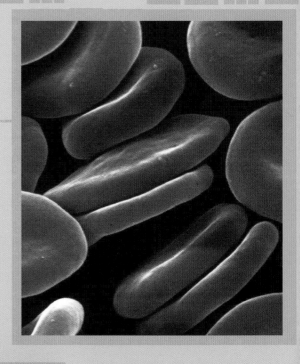

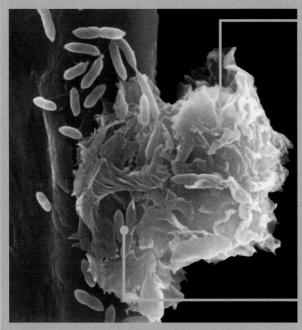

White blood cells travel with red blood cells. They hunt down germs that invade your body, such as these sausage-shaped **bacteria**. White blood cells defend you by swallowing enemies whole!

Muscle cells help you to move. They do this by getting shorter, or contracting. When a muscle cell is relaxed, it's long and stretchy. But when it contracts, it pulls together and gets shorter. The sudden shortening causes bones and other body parts to move.

Without nerve cells, muscle cells couldn't do a thing. **Nerve cells** are your body's great communicators. They gather information and send messages all around your body. Some of these messages tell muscles when to contract.

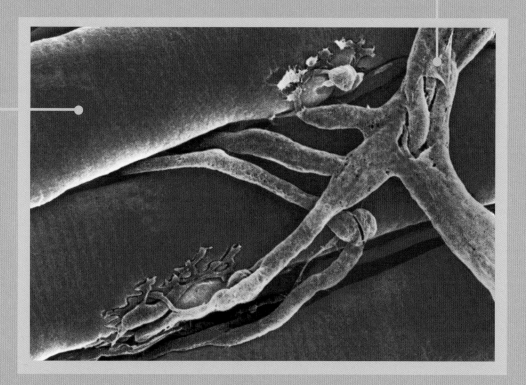

You have lots of nerve cells. Your brain has more than 100 billion! Nerve cells run down your backbone and reach into the tips of your fingers and toes.

Some nerve cells help you hear, see, taste, smell, or touch. Others allow you to sense heat, cold, and pressure. With these cells, you feel the chill of a cold wind, the warmth of the sun, and the hug of a friend.

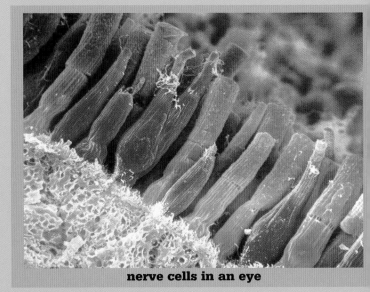

nerve cells in an eye

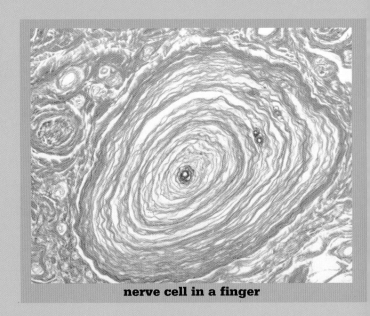

nerve cell in a finger

Your body has 206 bones. Every one of them is made up of millions of cells. It's hard to imagine cells that are hard. But **bone cells** surround themselves with a very hard substance called matrix that they make themselves. Your bones aren't as hard as rock. But they are strong enough to support the trillions of cells that make up the rest of you!

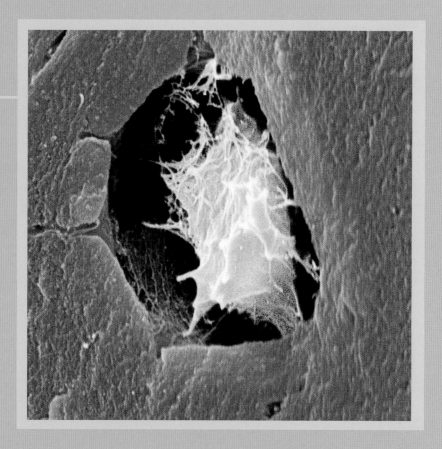

Body cells often work in teams. Groups of cells working together are called tissues.

Many muscle cells make up muscle tissue. And many nerve cells make up nervous tissue. A few types of skin cells together form epithelial tissue. **Epithelial tissue** covers the outside of your body. It also lines the inside of some body parts, such as your stomach and intestines.

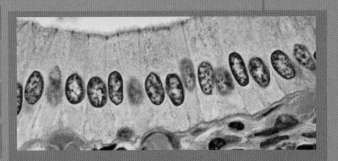

Connective tissue links and supports. It's usually made up of different kinds of cells and fibers. Stretchy **tendons** that connect muscles to bones are connective tissue. So are bone, fat, cartilage, and blood.

Groups of tissues that work together form organs. Your stomach is an organ. It's made of muscle tissue, nervous tissue, epithelial tissue, and connective tissue. Other organs include your brain, eyes, heart, and lungs—just to name a few.

Groups of organs work together in organ systems. Your circulatory system moves blood through your body. The digestive system breaks down the food you eat to give your body energy.

Your body's systems are very complex. They can do some amazing things. But they all start with the same building blocks. They all start with cells.

chapter 5
cells with special talents

You know that cell division turns one cell into many. Divisions produce enough cells to build an entire animal. But cell division doesn't stop, even when a body is fully formed. It continues throughout life.

Right now, cells in your body are dividing. New cells are added to your body as you grow. You can thank dividing bone cells for the fact that you're taller today than you were a year ago.

Cell division also replaces worn-out cells. Every day, millions of cells in your body die. But replacements are ready to take over.

Your skin is a perfect example. Give it a good scratch. Scratching makes lots of skin flakes, especially if your skin is dry. Those flakes are **dead skin cells**. Don't worry—losing skin cells is natural. Cell division makes new skin cells to replace the old ones. Your entire outer layer of skin is completely replaced every two to four weeks!

Red blood cells are even more amazing. The average red blood cell lives 120 days. By that time, it has traveled through your body about seventy-five thousand times.

Every second, your liver and spleen destroy 2.5 million red blood cells. At the same time, your body makes just as many new red blood cells by cell division. **New red blood cells** form constantly deep inside many of your bones.

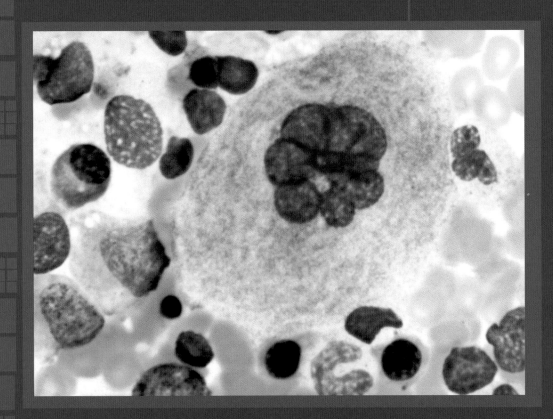

You need new cells when you get a cut or scrape in your skin. Cell division makes new cells near the injury. These new cells replace the cells that were destroyed. A scab forms over the injury. When the scab comes off, you see **brand-new skin**.

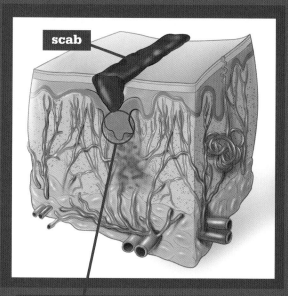

scab

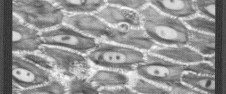

dividing cells

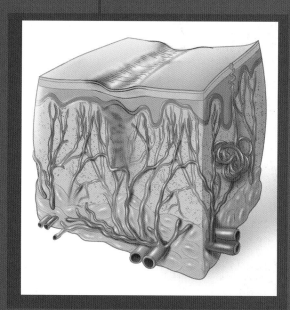

Thanks to cell division, cuts, scrapes, and many other kinds of wounds heal on their own. But if you lose a finger or a foot, it won't just grow back. There are limits to what normal cell division can do in humans.

Some other animals can replace lost body parts. This **sea star** had five big arms. It lost three. Brand-new arms are growing back to replace those arms. Some lizards can regrow lost tails. Growing back an entire arm or a tail is called regeneration. It takes a lot of cell divisions.

A **planarian** is only about 0.5 inch (1 centimeter) long. But it has a big talent for regeneration. If you cut one of these worms in half, each half will grow back into a whole worm. The bottom half will grow a new top, and the top half will grow a new bottom. If you split one lengthwise, the planarian will grow two heads!

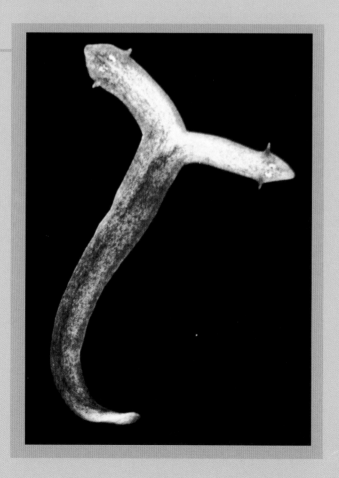

People will probably never match what sea stars and planarians can do. But many scientists think they can improve human powers of regeneration. How? By putting **stem cells** to work.

Stem cells are a unique kind of cell in your body. They are undifferentiated. That means they don't have a specific job to do. They can become any kind of cell in your body.

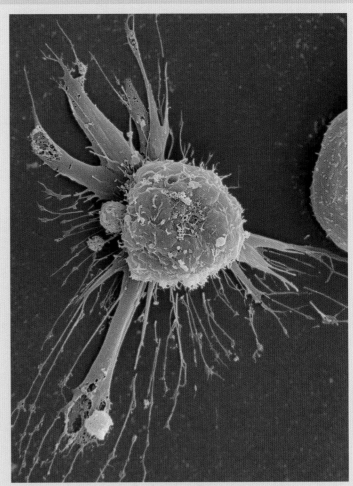

Imagine you are remodeling a house. The house needs many repairs. In your toolbox, you have a magic material that can change into whatever you need. It can become lumber, nails, carpet, shingles, or anything else. With this material, you can fix or build almost anything.

In your body, stem cells are like that magic material. If we can learn how to control stem cells, we could turn them into any kind of body cell. Those cells could be used to repair lost or damaged body parts.

One day, doctors might be able to use stem cells to treat other health problems. Examples include Alzheimer's disease (a disease of cells in the brain), spinal cord injuries, and liver disease. Stem cells might even be used to grow new organs to replace those that are damaged or worn out.

Stem cells are talented. But you have other cells in your body—called gametes—that can make more than just new cells. Gametes can make a new person.

In girls, gametes are egg cells. In boys, they are sperm. When you are older, if one of your **gametes** joins with its partner

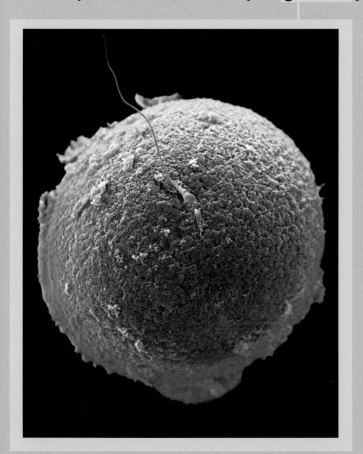

cell, it will be the start of another human being. That cell will begin to divide. And it will follow exactly the same path that your first cell did to become you.

The same is true for all the animals on earth. **From aardvarks to zebras—and everything in between—all animals begin as a single, mighty animal cell.**

glossary

amino acids: chemicals that are linked together to make proteins

cell: the smallest unit of life. Cells are building blocks of living things.

cell division: the process by which one cell divides to become two identical cells

cell membrane: the covering that surrounds a cell and controls what leaves and enters it

centrosomes: organelles that organize microtubules during cell division

chromosomes: structures in the nucleus of a cell that are made of DNA

connective tissue: a type of tissue in animal bodies that connects other tissues and forms packing and filling material in the body

contract: to pull together or shorten

cytosol: the salty gel that fills a cell and surrounds the cell's organelles

cytoskeleton: a supporting framework in cells that is made of fibers

daughter cells: the cells produced when a parent cell divides

deoxyribonucleic acid (DNA): the material in cells that carries the complete set of instructions for building an organism

differentiate: to become specialized to carry out a certain job

duplicated: copied exactly

egg: a cell that has half the number of chromosomes as a body cell. In animals, the female (mother) animal produces eggs.

embryo: a very early form of a developing animal

endoplasmic reticulum (ER): an organelle in cells that processes newly made proteins

epithelial tissue: a type of tissue in animal bodies that covers surfaces and lines some parts inside the body

fertilization: the process in which an egg and sperm join to make a new organism

gametes: egg and sperm cells

Golgi complex: an organelle in cells that processes and packages proteins

lysosomes: organelles in cells that help break down worn-out cell parts

matrix: a hard substance that bone cells make

microfilament: a threadlike structure that helps cells move

microtubule: a tubelike structure that provides support in a cell and moves organelles from place to place

mitochondria: organelles in cells that provide the power that cells need for everything they do

mitosis: cell division in which one parent cell divides into two identical daughter cells

nucleus: an organelle that contains a cell's DNA

organ: a body structure made up of different tissues that work together

organelle: a small structure that carries out a specific job inside a cell

parent cell: a cell that divides to produce two identical daughter cells

proteins: chemical substances that are the building blocks of cells. Proteins are made from chains of amino acids.

regeneration: regrowth of a tissue or body part that has been lost

ribosome: a cell organelle that strings together amino acids to make proteins

sperm: a cell that has half the number of chromosomes as a body cell. In animals, the male (father) animal produces sperm.

stem cells: cells that can develop into any type of specialized cell

tissue: a group of similar cells that work together

undifferentiated: cells that do not have a specific structure or function. Stem cells are undifferentiated.

vesicle: a small sac containing substances inside a cell

read more about animal cells

Books

Behler, John, and Debbie Behler. *Frogs: A Chorus of Colors.* New York: Sterling Publishing, 2005.

Beltz, Ellin. *Frogs: Inside Their Remarkable World.* Buffalo: Firefly Books, 2005.

Harris, Robie H. *It's So Amazing! A Book about Eggs, Sperm, Birth, Babies, and Families.* Cambridge, MA: Candlewick Press, 1999.

Levine, Shar, Leslie Johnstone, and Elaine Humphrey. *Extreme 3-D: Weird Animals.* Berkeley, CA: Silver Dolphin Books, 2006.

Websites

Cell City
http://www.biopic.co.uk/cellcity/index.htm
This British website takes you on a bus tour through an animal cell.

The Cell: Down to Basics
http://www.beyondbooks.com/lif71/4.asp
Read about the basics of cell structure and cell theory—the idea that all living things are made of cells.

Control of the Cell Cycle
http://nobelprize.org/educational_games/medicine/2001/
In this game, you're the cell division supervisor. Your job is to make sure that cell division goes smoothly.

Table of Contents: Cell Biology
http://www.cellsalive.com/toc_cellbio.htm
Click "Cell Models" to learn more about organelles. Click on "Mitosis" to watch an animated cell divide.

index

about the author

Rebecca L. Johnson is the author of many award-winning science books for children. Her previous books include the Biomes of North America series, *The Digestive System, The Muscular System, Genetics,* and *Plate Tectonics.* Ms. Johnson lives in Sioux Falls, South Dakota.

photo acknowledgments

The images in this book are used with the permission of: © Dr. Dennis Kunkel/Visuals Unlimited, pp. 6 (top), 11, 28 (bottom), 35; © Thomas Deerinck/Visuals Unlimited, pp. 6 (bottom), 19; © Biodisc/Visuals Unlimited, p. 7; © Dr. John D. Cunningham/Visuals Unlimited, pp. 8 (top), 36; © Biophoto Associates/Photo Researchers, Inc., pp. 8 (bottom), 37; © SPL/Photo Researchers, Inc., pp. 12, 31; © Professors Pietro M. Motta & Tomonori Naguro/Photo Researchers, Inc., p. 13 (top); © Dr. Fred Hossler/Visuals Unlimited, pp. 13 (bottom), 23 (bottom right); © Jennifer Waters/Photo Researchers, Inc., p. 14; © Dr. Donald W. Fawcett/Visuals Unlimited, pp. 15, 29; © Dr. Richard Kessel & Dr. Gene Shih/Visuals Unlimited, pp. 21, 23 (top); © Dwight R. Kuhn, pp. 22, 23 (bottom left); © Christian Darkin/Photo Researchers, Inc., p. 24; Wellcome Photo Library, p. 25; © Susumu Nishinaga/Photo Researchers, Inc., p. 27 (left); © Dr. David M. Phillips/Visuals Unlimited, pp. 27 (right), 28 (top); © Omikron/Photo Researchers, Inc., p. 30 (top); © Gene Cox/Photo Researchers, Inc., p. 30 (bottom); © Ed Reschke/Peter Arnold, Inc., p. 32 (top); © Biology Media/Photo Researchers, Inc., p. 32 (bottom); © David Wrobel/Visuals Unlimited, p. 38; © Tom Adams/Visuals Unlimited, p. 39; © David Scharf/Peter Arnold, Inc., p. 40; © Eye of Science/Photo Researchers, Inc., p. 43.

Front cover: © Gene Cox/Photo Researchers, Inc. (background), © Lerner Publishing Group, Inc. (illustration).